Flutter and Float

Bringing Home Goldfish

by Amanda Doering Tourville
illustrated by Andi Carter

Special thanks to our advisers for their expertise:

Sharon Hurley, D.V.M.
New Ulm (Minnesota) Regional
Veterinary Center

Terry Flaherty, Ph.D., Professor of English
Minnesota State University, Mankato

PiCTURE WiNDOW BOOKS
Minneapolis, Minnesota

Editor: Jill Kalz
Designer: Hilary Wacholz
Page Production: Michelle Biedscheid
Art Director: Nathan Gassman
Associate Managing Editor: Christianne Jones
The illustrations in this book were created with mixed media.
Photo Credit: Andrey Armyagov/Shutterstock, 23

Picture Window Books
151 Good Counsel Drive
P.O. Box 669
Mankato, MN 56002-0669
877-845-8392
www.picturewindowbooks.com

 All books published by Picture Window Books
are manufactured with paper containing at least
10 percent post-consumer waste.

Library of Congress Cataloging-in-Publication Data
Tourville, Amanda Doering, 1980-
Flutter and float : bringing home goldfish / by
Amanda Doering Tourville ; illustrated by Andi Carter.
p. cm. – (Get a pet)
Includes index.
ISBN 978-1-4048-4853-5 (library binding)
1. Goldfish–Juvenile literature. I. Carter, Andi, 1976- ill. II. Title.
SF458.G6T68 2009
639.3'7484–dc22   2008006425

Table of Contents

New Fish

Henry is getting pet fish! Several days before bringing them home, Henry sets up the fish tank. He pours gravel into the bottom of it. He and his dad prepare the water. They put in the filter. It's important for the water to be just right before putting fish into it.

Fish are fun to have as pets, but they're also a lot of work.
Is Henry ready?

TIP
Pet stores are the most common places to buy pet fish. Some cities also have special fish stores that sell only fish and fish supplies. Pick a place that has many fish to choose from.

Choosing Goldfish

Like most people, Henry is buying his fish from a pet store. Henry wants goldfish. Goldfish are hardy and easy to keep.

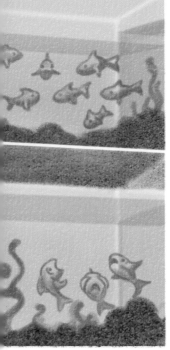

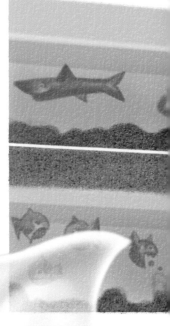

> **TIP**
> Make sure there aren't any dead fish floating in the store's tank. Dead fish can dirty the water and make the living fish sick.

Henry wants to pick out healthy goldfish. Healthy fish are active. Their gills move easily. Their eyes are clear. Their scales and fins are clean, smooth, and free of white spots.

Henry names his goldfish Betty, Bubbles, and Bob.

Coming Home

Henry's new goldfish are home! But they are a little scared. Everything is new to them.

Henry doesn't take his goldfish out of the bags right away. First, he slowly lowers the bags into the tank. He gives the goldfish a chance to get used to the water temperature. After 20 minutes, Henry carefully opens the bags and tips them. His fish swim out into the tank.

TIP
Once your fish are in their tank, turn off the lights. Leave the fish alone for about an hour so they can settle into their new home.

Time to Eat

Once a day, Henry feeds his goldfish special fish food. The food looks like small flakes. Henry watches to see how much food his fish can eat in five minutes. That's the amount he feeds them every day.

TIP
Overfeeding is a common problem with pet fish. Too much food can make the fish sick. It can also make the water and tank dirty.

Goldfish like treats once in a while. Dried bloodworms or brine shrimp are good choices. Henry buys his fish food and treats at the pet store.

Keeping Clean

Henry has to help clean the house. He also has to help clean his pets' house! Once a week, Henry and his dad clean the gravel in the fish tank. They use a gravel cleaner they got at the pet store. It sucks up leftover food and fish waste.

Next, Henry and his dad change about one-fifth of the water. They make sure the new water they put in is warm. Changing water helps keep the fish tank clean.

TIP
A filter also keeps the water in your fish tank clean. A filter sucks in water and traps harmful chemicals and waste. The cleaned water goes back into the tank.

Safe Water

Henry and his dad make sure the water in the fish tank is safe. They test it once a week with a test kit. Every time they add water to the tank, they condition it. Pet stores sell special water test kits and conditioning drops.

Henry checks the water temperature every day. He doesn't want his goldfish to get too hot or too cold. He uses a thermometer that sticks to the side of the tank.

TIP

Different fish live best at different temperatures. A goldfish's water should be between 68 and 72 degrees Fahrenheit (20 and 22 Celsius). This is about how warm your house is.

Staying Healthy

Fish can get sick, so Henry checks his goldfish every day. He makes sure they are active and eating well. He checks their scales for white spots. White spots mean a fish is sick.

If Henry thinks one of his goldfish is sick, he takes him to a veterinarian. The vet checks the fish and answers Henry's questions. She may send medicine home with Henry. Fish stores are good places to get help for sick fish, too.

TIP
The most important thing you can do to keep your fish healthy is to make sure the water is clean. Many fish illnesses are caused by dirty water.

Good Night, Goldfish!

Fish don't sleep like people, but they do rest. When Henry's goldfish are resting, they often sit near the bottom of the tank. They don't move much.

Henry keeps his fish tank away from windows or doors that can let in cold air. He keeps it away from sunlight, too. The sun can heat the water and hurt the goldfish.

TIP
Keep your fish tank in a safe, quiet place. Goldfish don't like loud noises.

Happy Pets

Fish are great pets. They are quiet and a lot of fun to watch. If Henry takes good care of his goldfish, he may have his swimming friends for 10 years or more!

Goldfish Close-up

A goldfish's **EYES** are on both sides of its head.

A goldfish smells through its **NOSTRILS**. Goldfish have a very good sense of smell.

A goldfish's **SCALES** help protect its body.

A goldfish breathes through its **GILLS**. The gills take in oxygen from the water.

FINS help a goldfish swim and change direction.

A goldfish waves its **TAIL** back and forth to swim forward.

Goldfish Life Cycle

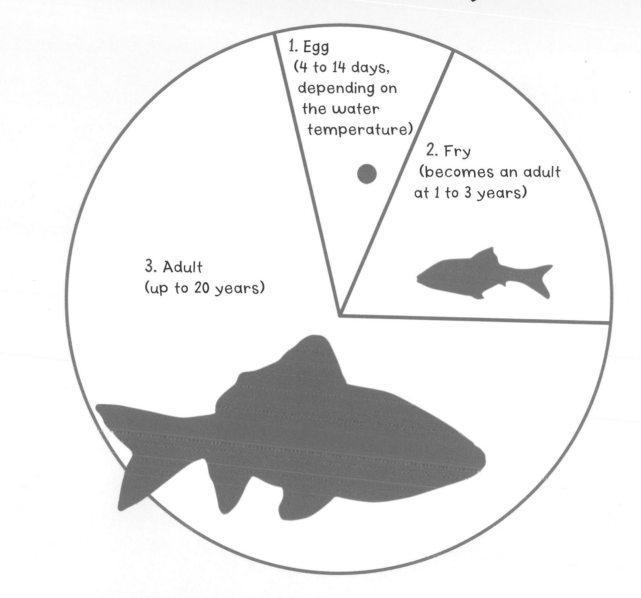

1. Egg
(4 to 14 days, depending on the water temperature)

2. Fry
(becomes an adult at 1 to 3 years)

3. Adult
(up to 20 years)

Glossary

condition—to remove harmful chemicals

gills—part of a fish that helps it breathe underwater

gravel—small rocks

scales—small pieces of tough skin that cover the bodies of some animals, including fish and snakes

veterinarian—a doctor who takes care of animals; vet, for short

Goldfish

To Learn More

More Books to Read

Binns, Tristan Boyer. *Freshwater Fish.* Chicago: Heinemann Library, 2006.

Buckmaster, Marjorie L. *Freshwater Fishes.* New York: Marshall Cavendish Benchmark, 2007.

Goodbody, Slim. *Goldfish.* Pleasantville, N.Y.: Gareth Stevens Pub., 2008.

Richardson, Adele. *Caring for Your Fish.* Mankato, Minn.: Capstone Press, 2007.

On the Web

FactHound offers a safe, fun way to find Web sites related to topics in this book. All of the sites on FactHound have been researched by our staff.

1. Visit *www.facthound.com*
2. Type in this special code: 1404848533
3. Click on the FETCH IT button.

Your trusty FactHound will fetch the best sites for you!

Index

Look for all of the books in the Get a Pet series:

Flutter and Float: Bringing Home Goldfish
Purr and Pounce: Bringing Home a Cat
Scurry and Squeak: Bringing Home a Guinea Pig
Skitter and Scoot: Bringing Home a Hamster
Twitter and Tweet: Bringing Home a Bird
Woof and Wag: Bringing Home a Dog